Mama Hoa's
Vietnamese Specialty Cuisine

A memoir and brief collection of unique
Vietnamese Recipes

By Gordon Lawry

Title: Mama Hoa's Vietnamese Specialty Cuisine

Author: Gordon Lawry

Illustrations by: Lulie Lawry May

Recipe Translation: Sandra Leigh Lawry

This personal recipe booklet is dedicated to Ms. Hoa Nguyen.

Hoa Nguyen Pensacola Beach 2003

Our Vietnamese Grandmother

When Hoa was a new mother with a young child, she fled Saigon for America during the Vietnam War. Her husband was sent to a re-education camp in Vietnam and Hoa began her life in America, never to see her husband again.

With the help of her dear friend from church, Chloe Lawry (my mother) Hoa learned English. Hoa was fluent in French so Chloe taught Hoa English by speaking French. Hoa was a close family friend for many years beginning in the 1980s. Hoa enjoyed lovingly preparing and serving these dishes to our family on many occasions, and we were always beyond amazed at her cooking. Throughout her life in America, Hoa opened a successful Vietnamese restaurant in Northern Virginia while raising her daughter and gaining American Citizenship.

Initially published as a simple family tribute to Hoa, this short and simple recipe book is indeed a collection of recipes for her best Vietnamese dishes. However, just as importantly, it provides humorous stories and anecdotes about Hoa that highlight her as our wonderful and devoted friend, a dedicated and loving mother, and a gifted culinary wizard.

I sincerely hope you enjoy these fun stories about Hoa and the simple but amazing recipes.

Vietnamese cuisine is well known for using fresh ingredients, compelling spices, and incredible flavor. But mostly the love and devotion to family and friends is what always make these times so precious!

Enjoy!

CONTENTS

CRAB-ASPARAGUS SOUP

Ingredients

- Chicken stock
- Tapioca starch
- Water to thicken the stock
- Crabmeat
- Dash fish sauce
- 1 tsp. Sugar
- 2 Egg yolks
- Black pepper or White pepper

Directions

1. Stir in starch to thicken stock.
2. Beat egg yolk, slowly pour into gently boiling stock.
3. Stir with chopsticks quickly to cook egg in small pieces.
4. Add Asparagus & crab.

Delicious!!

HOA'S PICKLED VEGGIES

Ingredients

- 1 cup Vinegar - white
- 2 ½ cups Water
- 1 Tb. Salt
- 1 cup Sugar

Directions

1. Simmer.
2. Add carrots, cabbage, bok choy, cauliflower, baby corn, onions, etc.

CHOW

Ingredients & Directions

Large Rice Vermicelli
1. Boiled 3 min
2. Rinse in cold water
3. Place over bed of Romaine and mint sliced thin
4. Place cucumber rounds on edge

Sauté:
Garlic, slivers of red onion, small pieces pork for 10 min or until cooked.

Add:
Diced Peanuts (Yue) to noodles and place meat mixture over all.

Serve with Nuc Moum!

STEAMED FISH

Ingredients

- 3 Fish steaks - firm
- Garlic
- Black pepper
- Sugar
- Paprika
- 1½ can "Temple" black beans
- Shitake mushrooms - soaked
- Rice noodles (bean) drained
- Green onion pieces

Directions

1. Drizzle with corn oil.
2. Steam 20 min.

FRESH SALAD SPRING ROLL

Ingredients

- Rice paper - moistened
- Rice Noodles - cooked
- Lettuce
- Cilantro - mint
- Matchstick cucumber and/or bean sprouts
- Shredded chicken
- Pork loin
- Butterfly Shrimp

Directions

1. Roll all into rice papers.

Dip in Sauce:

1. 3 tsp. Hoisin sauce
2. ½ Tb. peanut butter
3. Dash hot water - chili paste

EGG ROLL

Once Hoa decided to come visit us in Pensacola FL. We had planned the trip for the best weather which is generally springtime. After a few phone calls back and forth, Hoa called to announce that she was coming to visit! She excitedly proclaimed that by stating "I come to your house eggroll". Having emotions of joy about her coming but confusion regarding when she would come, I replied "Great Hoa, when are you planning to come?". Again, Hoa announced, "I come to your house eggroll!"

Somewhat bewildered at her second response I attempted to confirm the time of her visit once again with Hoa by asking "Are you coming to visit?" She replied, "Gordon, I upset you", which meant she was upset with me. I asked her why. Hoa replied, "I tell you again; I come to your house egg roll", but this time she added, "January, February, March, Eggroll!". Oh, I said. April, you are coming in April! Hoa exclaimed, "YES! I tell you three times, I come to your house in eggroll!" To this day, when our family discusses anything in April, invariably the words "eggroll" come up!

CHICKEN SOUP STOCK

Ingredients

Broth:

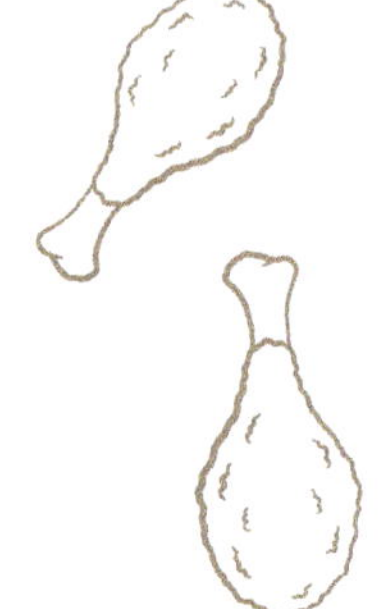

- 1 gal. Water
- 2 Chopped leeks Zc.
- 1½ cups Thin sliced fresh ginger
- 1 cup Chopped celery
- 3 Tb. Fish sauce
- 1Tsp. Black peppercorn
- 10 Chicken wings
- 8 Chicken legs
- 2 Bunches cilantro
- 2 Bay leaves
- 1 Sweet onion, quartered

Directions

1. Combine all and bring to boil.
2. Simmer 3hours, strain.

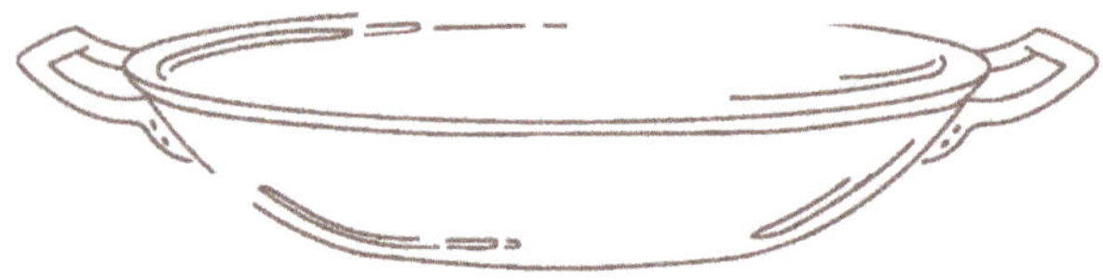

<u>**Add for Soup:**</u>

- Clear noodles or rice noodles, softened
- Shredded chix breast
- White Pepper
- Red chillies
- Cilantro
- Thai basil
- Lime wedges

*Nuc Moum (Optional)

LEMONGRASS SHRIMP WITH RICE VERMICELLI AND VEGGIES

"Bun Tom Nuong X2"

In Ziploc Bag Add:

- $1/3$ cup Fish sauce
- ¼ cup Sugar
- 2 Tb. Chopped fresh Lemongrass (only pale bottom part of stalk)
- 1 Tb. Veg. oil
- 2 Cloves chopped garlic
- 32 Large peeled, deveined Shrimp & marinate 1 hour in fridge

Make Shallot Oil

- ¾ cup chopped shallots
- ¼ cup veg. oil
- Sauté 5 min till brown.

Directions

1. Place 8 oz. rice vermicelli in boiling water for 20 min.
2. Drain & combine with:

- Shallots
- 1 ¾ cups Lettuce, Boston
- 1 cup Bean sprouts
- 1 cup Shredded carrot
- 1 med. Cucumber, thin sliced halves

3. Toss well.
4. Grill Shrimp 2 ½ min per side
5. Place noodle mix in bowl, top with shrimp, fried shallots.

<u>Serve with Extra</u>

Lettuce
Carrots
Mint
Chopped peanuts
Nuc Moum (optional)

CITIZENSHIP TEST

After studying and being tutored in English for a few years, Hoa decided to apply for American Citizenship. So, she enrolled in classes that she dutifully attended for the required time all the while being assisted by Chloe's supplemental instruction in English.

Finally, the big day came and Hoa was on her way to the Citizenship test. The story, as told by my brother Donelson, goes like this. Chloe was driving while Donelson and Hoa were both passengers in the back seat. Chloe handed Donelson a sheet of paper with some of the anticipated citizenship test topics and requested Donelson to ask Hoa a few questions to help prepare her for the test.

So, Donelson began to drill Hoa on a few questions:

Donelson: "Hoa, who was the first American President?"

Hoa: "Oh, I know, I know, Abraham Lincoln!"

Donelson: "No, it was George Washington."

Hoa: "Oh yea, yea George Washington."

Donelson: "Hoa, when was the American Civil War?"

Hoa "I know, I know, 1775!"

Donelson: "No, it was in 1861, the American Revolutionary War was in 1775!"

 "Let's try another one. How many original colonies were there in America?"

Hoa, "I know I know, fifty!"

Donelson "No there were thirteen colonies, there are fifty states now."

This went on for a while with Hoa knowing dates and names but with some confusion regarding which date/name went with which question.

Despite this Chloe proclaimed "If I know Hoa and her stubbornness, then there is one thing I can tell you for sure, Hoa is coming out of that test with her American Citizenship". Sure enough, an hour later Hoa emerged from the test with a huge grin on her face and a spring in her step! "I did it" she proclaimed!

FRIED RICE

<u>Ingredients & Directions</u>

½ cup Sunlee sweet rice (cooked)

<u>*The Asian way is to put dry Rice in pan</u>:

Fill with water to the first knuckle of your finger, from top of rice, bring to boil, turn down to low and put cover on, 20 min.

<u>Sauté in Oil:</u>

- Peanut or sesame
- ¼ White onion, sliced thin
- 1 Green onion ½" cut
- Chinese Sausage sliced thin
- I small Pork "Saushu" sliced thin
- 1 ½ Oyster sauce
- ¼ cup Shrimps
- 1 Tb. Sugar

Add sautéd mix to RICE - ENJOY!

BUN PAO

Ingredients & Directions

- 6 oz. Self Rising flour
- 1-2 Tb. Baking powder
- ¼ cup Sugar

Stir together.

Stir in:

- ¼ cup peanut oil
- 1 cup milk

Filling

-
- ¾ cup Diced cabbage
- 1/8 cup Sliced mushrooms
- ¼ cup Green onions
- 1 cup Ground pork
- 1/8 cup Chinese suasage, chopped
- 1 ½ Tb. Sugar
- 1 ½ Tb. Oyster sauce
- Tad black pepper
- 1 tsp. Flour
- 1 tsp. Sesame oil

Blend, make small meatball and place in flour ball.

Steam 15-20 min.

BEEF AND RICE NOODLE SOUP
"Pho Bo"

Ingredients

Broth:

- 3 lbs. Beef oxtail
- ¾ cup Thin sliced fresh ginger
- ²/³ cup Chopped shallots
- 5 Qtr. Water
- 4 cups Chopped claikon
- 2 Tb. Sugar
- 3 Tb. Fish Sauce
- 1 tsp. White peppercorns
- 5 Whole cloves
- 2 Star anise
- 1 Yellow onion, quartered
- 1 Cinnamon stick

Directions

1. Saute first 3.
2. Add water and next 8.
3. Bring to boil; simmer 4 Hours. Strain.
4. Put Broth in large pot. Heat on low.

<u>Add for Soup:</u> (to each bowl)

- Rice vermicelli softened in boiled water
- Sliced onion or green onions
- Fresh bean sprouts
- Sliced Eye of Round pieces
- Cilantro
- Thai basil
- Lime wedges
- Nuc Moum (optional)

GREEN PAPAYA SALAD
"Goi Du Du"

Ingredients

- ½ cup Lime juice
- ¼ cup Sugar
- 3 Tb. Fish Sauce
- 4 cups Julienne-cut peeled Papaya
- 3 cups Match-cut carrots
- 2 Red Thai chiles seeded, sliced thin
- $2/3$ cup Chopped cilantro
- ¼ cup Chopped peanuts

Directions

1. Add first 3 ingredients in bowl, whisk together.
2. Add papaya, carrots, chilles, toss well.
3. Let stand 20 min, sprinkle with cilantro & peanuts.

NOT TOO SMALL

While visiting Pensacola from Northern Virginia one summer, Hoa engaged in one of her favorite outdoor pastimes; crabbing. We had gone crabbing around Solomons Island Maryland in the past and Hoa proved herself very proficient at catching crabs and more importantly, preparing them in delectable dishes like Crab-Asparagus soup!

One requirement in the State of Florida regarding crabbing is that they must be a minimum size to keep. This is normally not an issue as long as the crabbing takes place in summer which allows the crabs to grow to a suitable (legal) size.

One afternoon in late spring, Hoa went down to the dock to do some crabbing. I joined her several hours later and noticed that she had acquired quite a haul already. After inspecting her catch, I informed her that two crabs were too small to keep. Hoa replied, "No, not too small, very sweet!" Realizing that Hoa thought I was commenting on the crabs' suitability for eating and not their legality, I tried again. However, Hoa again said "Crabs OK, very sweet!" After a few more back-and-forth attempts at clarification, I finally acquiesced. There was no convincing Hoa once she had her mind made up. Indeed, they were some of the best crabs we've ever had!

HOA'S VIETNAMESE CURRY

Ingredients & Directions

In a bowl:
- 5-6 Pieces chicken
- 2 Tb. Dry curry (D-D Madras curry)
- 2 Bay leaves
- 2 Tb. Sugar
- 1 Tb. Salt

Mix all and let stand.

In large pot:
2 Tb. oil heated and saute chicken on medium.

Add:
1 Tb. Ketchup
½ Onion sliced
4 Potatoes diced
4 Carrots diced

Simmer 10 min.

Add:
1 ¼ Tb. (D-D GOLD) curry paste
1 tsp. Butter
1/2 cup Water

Simmer 10 min.

Add:
4 oz. Sour cream
7-8 oz. Milk
(Lulie substitutes coconut milk for this!)

SPARKY THE DOG

Hoa had a wonderful daughter and three grandchildren during her time in America. Hoa would go visit and stay with their family from time to time and would report on all activities that had occurred with her family in Northern Virginia. Once, while talking about her grandchildren she mentioned how happy they were with Bucky their new dog She explained how Bucky would jump and play with the children and was such a fun part of the family. Over the next few months, we would periodically get updates on how the grandchildren were doing and of course Bucky.

At one point I met with Hoa's daughter Kim and told her how much we enjoyed hearing about the grandchildren and Bucky.

Kim, with a rather puzzled look on her face, replied, "Who is Bucky?"

I said "Hoa had told us that you had a new dog and how much fun he was".

Kim exclaimed, "Oh, you must mean Sparky! We have a great dog named Sparky!"

HOA'S WON TON SOUP

Ingredients

- 1# gr. Pork or chicken
- ½ cup Green onion minced
- ½ cup Shrimp chopped
- 5 White mushrooms chopped
- 1 tsp. Sugar
- 1 Tb. Nuc moum
- ½ tsp. Sesame oil
- Black pepper

Directions

1. Mix all in bowl.
2. Pinch small ball to fit in Wonton wrapper.
3. Put water on fingers and on wrapper edges and pleat to close.
4. Boil until floating.
5. Remove and cool, store in fridge.

To place in hot chicken broth: Use garnish white onion with green onion, or as desired.

(Thin sliced cabbage or greens, black mushroom are good!)

CHIA GIÁ

Ingredients

Vietnamese Egg Roll:

- 2 lbs. Ground pork
- 3 Carrots - shredded & squeeze)
- ¾ cup Chopped mushroom - any kind
- ½ small Cabbage shredded
- 1 can Crab - small can or shrimp
- 1 medium Onion diced
- 3 Tb. Sugar
- 2 oz Clear noodles, bean thread
- ½ cup Fish sauce
- 1-2 tsp. Pepper
- 50 lumpia wrappers -layered in damp towel while using

Directions

1. Mix all and wrap in Egg Roll style, tightly.
2. Fry in shallow cast iron pan on medium high to medium heat turning till brown.
3. Remove to drain on paper towels.

Serve with lettuce, mint, Rau Ram, cilantro around Roll if desired and Nuc Moum!

NUC MOUM

"Vietnamese dipping sauce"

Ingredients

- 2 Cloves garlic
- 3 tsp. Sugar
- Juice of 1 lemon
- 1 cup Fish sauce
- 2 tsp. Red chillie
- Water to desired taste

Directions

1. Put all in a sealable jar or Soy Sauce type jar.
2. Store in fridge.

www.ingramcontent.com/pod-product-compliance
Lightning Source LLC
Chambersburg PA
CBHW041939110726
48010CB00003B/156